IMAGES
of America

KEYPORT

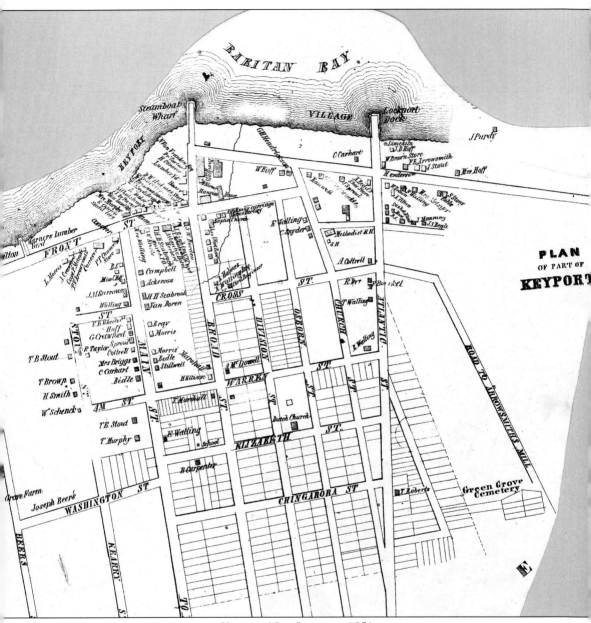

Keyport, New Jersey, in 1851.

IMAGES
of America

KEYPORT

Timothy E. Regan

ARCADIA

First published 1995
Copyright © Timothy E. Regan, 1995

ISBN 0-7524-0242-0

Published by Arcadia Publishing,
an imprint of the Chalford Publishing Corporation
One Washington Center, Dover, New Hampshire 03820
Printed in Great Britain

Library of Congress Cataloging-in-Publication Data applied for

Dedicated in the loving memory of my grandmother,
Gladys Virginia Evans Regan

Contents

Acknowledgments

It would have been impossible to create this historical volume without the help of the following people: my mother, Betty, for her inspiration and for instilling in me a desire to preserve history; my father, Gene, who took the time over and over to answer my questions of "What used to be there," or "Do you remember . . ."; Patricia Schleicher, for her love, guidance, patience, typing speed, and grammatical awareness; Norrine Schanck, curator of the Keyport Historical Society; Geraldine Brown Sentell and her late husband Doug "Scoop" Sentell; Fay Bennett and the late Albert Bennett, who I have to thank for my original interest in the research of Keyport history; Dave Galloway for his assistance and friendship; John Reith for help and enthusiasm with the project; Lincoln Hose Co. No. 1; and all of my friends who helped with this project.

A very special thank you goes to Bertram Morris. Without Bert's guidance, enthusiasm, and willingness to loan the best photographs in his collection, I would never have succeeded with this project. Thank you Bert.

Introduction

The history of Keyport can be traced back to around 1664, when the area known as Chingarora, or "Fishing Point," was still a stopping place for Lenni Lenape Indians. In 1714 John Bowne, an original Monmouth patentee from 1670, sold 140 acres to Thomas and Michael Kearny, two merchant brothers from New York. The land was described as laying at Chingarora, commencing at the mouth of Lupakitongue Creek and running south by west up the creek towards the bay. The tract to the west was then known as Brown's Point, a small settlement at the mouth of the Matawan Creek which had been in existence since about 1700.

By 1717, Michael sold his shares to Thomas, who soon built Key Grove Farm atop Wolf Pit Hill. Thomas moved from New York to Key Grove Farm with his wife Catherine and several of their five children. Soon he was running sloops loaded with oysters and other produce to the island of Manhattan. Thomas passed away in 1747, at which time the land was willed to his son, Major James Kearny. James was involved in laying out Broadway Avenue from Middletown Point (Matawan) to Brown's Point in 1750. (It was at the Brown's Point wharf, now lower Broadway, that the first group of Revolutionary War soldiers boarded sloops and embarked to Long Island in 1773.) Major Kearny passed away around 1774, and the property was deeded to his brother Edmund. After Edmund's death in 1822, his twenty-one-year-old son, James Philip, became the heir of the estate. Unfortunately, James Philip did not possess much business sense, and by 1823 he had mortgaged a large part of the property to William Forman. In 1829, James Philip Kearny was forced to convey all of his rights and titles to Daniel and John W. Holmes, for the purpose of clearing the title and paying off the debts on the estate.

On November 3, 1829, the Orphans Court held a "Public Outcry and Vendue" at the Brown's Point Tavern for the purpose of a sale. The sale was advertised as "781 acres, Dwelling House, Kitchen, Barn, Wagon House, etc. Near Brown's Point Cove. Best harbor on the Raritan Bay. Of the 781 acres, 350 acres are woodland; the residue are able land and meadow." So on November 3–4, 1829, Key Grove Farm was divided, and after 115 years the property ceased being in the Kearny family. Fifteen separate lots were made and the sale totaled $19,941.19.

By April 1830, twenty-four lots were surveyed by Leonard Walling, and in February 1831 a road was laid out from Middletown Village to the new port. Also in April 1830, several business-minded men purchased sixteen lots with the intent of forming a dock company, and within several weeks the Key Port Company was created. The name was formed by taking "Key" from the "Key Grove" plantation and "Port" from what the company planned to do with the property.

The Key Port Company was responsible for building the first dock and storehouse in 1831. By 1832 the first hotel, the Atlantic, was built on the south side of Front Street, where it remained until 1877. Stage travel began by 1833, and soon routes such as Morrel's Line and others traveled from the docks to Middletown Point and further west to Freehold. In 1860, the *Keyport Express* was begun by J.H. Silsby and Co., becoming the village's first newspaper. The *Weekly Star* was formed in 1866, and in 1871 was bought by Dr. Wilmer Hodgson, who renamed it the *Keyport Weekly*. By 1879 the *Keyport Enterprise* was established by the Armstrong Brothers. Stores and houses began to spring up and Key Port began to look quite different from the old village of Chingarora.

The name Key Port was used as two words for many years. The village was at first governed by the Key Port Company from 1830 until 1848, at which time it became part of Raritan (Hazlet) Township. On March 17, 1870, Keyport broke away from Raritan Township and became a separate entity. It was governed by five elected commissioners: Rufus Ogden was chosen as the first mayor, and T.S.R. Brown, Captain Christian D. Emson, John S. Sproul, and Peter Hulse were the other original commissioners. This form of government remained until 1908, when Keyport became a borough.

Today this small port on the great bay retains much of its old world charm. Tranquil tree-lined streets obscure historic houses and churches. Boats still ply the waters where steamboats did in the nineteenth century, and people still fish the waters waiting for the big catch. One can take a quiet stroll through the Green Grove Cemetery, which holds many of the town's finest citizens, who may still be watching over the place they loved.

In retrospect, Keyport's history is unique: it has been in the making for nearly three hundred years, and I have made every attempt to spotlight the historical events, places, and people that have been important to this small town's past. Fortunately, several excellent sources were available to provide the historical data contained herein. They include: *The 100th Anniversary of the Keyport Weekly* (1969); *The 100th Anniversary of Keyport* (1930), by Josie Brown; Ellis' *History of Monmouth County* (1886); *The Bicentennial Book of Keyport* (1976), compiled by Vera Conover and Norrine Schanck; and finally, the Keyport Public Library microfilm collection from 1877 to 1972. Unfortunately, very few of the dates and other data correspond from one source to another. When doubt arose, I chose the most common, or I attempted to research the event in microfilm.

It is important for people to remember that the life we live today, becomes our history tomorrow. I hope you enjoy experiencing Keyport's past as much as I enjoyed writing it.

TIMOTHY E. REGAN
1995

One

Houses

The earliest dwellings built on the land we now know as Keyport were constructed by the Minisink Indians as early as the fifteenth century. Upon purchasing 140 acres in 1714, Thomas Kearny set about building Key Grove Farm atop Wolf Pit Hill along the "Lupakitongue Creek." Other places of dwelling quickly rose throughout the area known as Fishing Point, along the bay. The east tenant house of Key Grove Farm may have been built as early as 1745. This structure still stands on little Snyder Lane, despite the fact that, during the Revolution, British warships used this house for cannon practice from the bay. Nimrod Bedle built the first house in Keyport after it became a village in 1830. This house also still stands, on Main Street. By 1835 there were twelve houses in Keyport, and seventy by 1846. For the next century, Keyport became home to virtually every type of architectural style, including Early Colonial, Federal, Greek Revival, and Victorian. Today many of these structures have been restored, while others await an unknown fate, as so many other fine Keyport dwellings have.

THE KEY GROVE FARMHOUSE, 1717–1719. This unique structure was built in several stages starting in 1717. Indentured servants worked day and night to build the house for Thomas Kearny and his family. Lumber came from nearby forests and was hewn by hand on the spot, while bricks were formed of clay and mud and then sunbaked near the shore of the creek. Home to over three generations of Kearnys, it was finally sold and the vast farm was subdivided into building lots in 1829. The building remained a single family home throughout the nineteenth and early twentieth centuries. Early in the 1970s, the building was partially destroyed by fire. Two hundred and fifty-six years after its construction, the true cornerstone of Keyport was razed by a single bulldozer. The Keyport Historical Society has the original massive entrance doors and several mantelpieces from the house in its archives. Today the ten-story American Legion Apartment building stands on what is left of little Wolf Pit Hill, overlooking Luppatacong Creek.

THE BROWN'S POINT TAVERN, *c.* 1794. Jacobus Morrell purchased a tract of land from Major James Kearny and soon built this fine tavern and dwelling. In 1819 Morrell died, and his widow married Septimus Stevens. Stevens and his wife raised several children in this house and operated the tavern into the 1870s. The building was remodeled several times and in later years became a nursing home. It was destroyed by fire around 1975.

MAJOR JAMES PHILIP KEARNY'S HOUSE, *c.* 1772. James Philip married Agnes Watson Freneau in June 1771. Miss Watson was the mother of the renowned Revolutionary War poet Philip Freneau. This house was built to replace the former residence which was destroyed by fire in May 1772. Records of the old Morristown church indicate a death, of an infant, in the Kearny family in June 1772; it is quite possible this child was killed in the burning of the original mansion.

FRONT STREET, *c.* 1799. This house, which has since been razed, was for many years one of the oldest structures in Brown's Point. It most likely served as a tenant house for a farmhand on Key Grove Farm. The small upper windows attest to the very low, almost loft-like upper stories in eighteenth-century houses.

THE JOHN SNYDER HOUSE, *c.* 1805 This plain one-and-a-half-story frame dwelling was built on the corner of First and Church Streets. It was home to the first Methodist Sunday school class in Keyport. The small wing to the west has a very Dutch-like roof line. The building and the eighteenth-century barns were demolished in 1931, shortly after this photograph was taken.

NIMROD AND MARY BEDLE, 1860. Nimrod Bedle was born 2 miles south of Keyport in 1806. On January 3, 1829, he married Mary Forman and moved into the house below in 1831. Mr. Bedle was a farmer and fisherman by trade. He and his wife raised seven children in their Main Street home, which was also the home of the first Methodist church service in the new village.

NIMROD BEDLE'S HOUSE, 1831. Mr. Bedle built his home on Main Street shortly after the village was formed in 1830. His wife Susan soon gave birth to a son, John Rogers, the first baby to be born in the new town. It is thought that the original house was near the rear of the present house and may have been altered around 1850.

THE HOUSE OF ASHER COLLINS, *c.* 1838. This residence was originally built on Church Street, near John Street. It was moved by horse around 1900 to a lot on First Street, where it stands today virtually unchanged. Note the Gothic window in the attic dormer; this type of window became an common feature of nineteenth-century frame architecture. Many unexplained events have occurred at this residence, leading one to guess it may be haunted.

BROADWAY, *c.* 1840. This house is thought to have been the old Brown's Point Schoolhouse. It stood on the corner of West Second and Broadway until it was destroyed by a series of arson fires in 1993. A new house has been built which retains the lines of the former structure.

14

THE BAY VIEW HOUSE, c. 1853. Constructed on a bluff overlooking the Raritan Bay, this house was built by Joseph E. Coffee. The addition to the left was built with material from the steamboat *Troy*, using the windows, stairs, and even the stateroom doors in the master bedroom. In later years it was used by St. Mary's Church as a summer home for the ministry. The building was vacated in the 1970s and destroyed by fire around 1981. Condominiums now occupy the site.

THE WILLIAM H. WALLING HOUSE, c. 1869. A fine example of Second Empire-style architecture, this house stood on First Street, overlooking the bay. A common element of this architectural style was the center pavilion, which here rises to a mansard-roofed tower. In later years, it became a boarding house for the many seasonal residents seeking "good salt air." The house was razed in 1982, after being damaged in the Keyport Yacht Club fire.

THE METHODIST PARSONAGE, 1846. Soon after his term began, Reverend Burrowes built this fine frame house on Osborn Street. In 1856, the new church was erected on the southern lot, which to this day casts a shadow on the parsonage.

THE REFORMED PARSONAGE, 1862. Built on the grounds of the church, at the corner of Division and Osborn Streets, this house still serves the congregation and its minister. Its simple four-bay construction is common, but the offset doorway is unusual in this style.

GLAYDS VIRGINIA EVANS REGAN,
1903. Ms. Evans was born to Samuel and
Catherine Evans in their home on Second and
Fulton Streets in 1903. In 1921 she became
one of the first women to graduate from
Keyport High School, and she later worked at
the Aeromarine Corporation. She married
John Regan of Cliffwood and raised two
children in the house she purchased herself on
Spring Street.

GREENGROVE AVENUE, *c.* 1867. This
small wooden dwelling was built in the
Lockport section of town by the Ellison family.
Its unusual protruding dormers reflect a very
low ceiling height, in the days when tall
people were the minority.

THE BROWN HOUSE, *c.* 1871. This fine house was built in the Gothic style, to reflect the new public school that was just completed across the street. Note the elaborate porch rails, columns, and woodwork. The white picket fence was standard for almost all houses in town until the 1930s. This building remains a private dwelling in a time when many other houses of this size have been converted to professional purposes.

THE CAPTAIN WALLING HOUSE, *c.* 1847. Built in the Greek Revival style, this house is a characteristic "Brooklyn Row House." It may have been inspired by a ship captain or builder from New York, who brought this very unique urban design to the new village. Note the Ionic scrollwork in the window cornices and the heavily-boxed eaves.

THE HOUSES AT 55, 57, AND 59 SECOND STREET. These three homes were built in succession, from left to right, *c.* 1840, *c.* 1870, and *c.* 1885. All three houses still stand, although extensively remodeled.

CROSS (THIRD) STREET, *c.* 1845. The round attic window, large arched window, and protruding bay all combined to make this house one of the finest frame dwellings in town. When built, it overlooked the stream which ran from Necius Pond into the Raritan Bay and fed the Bedle Mill.

NO. 69 BROADWAY, *c.* 1860. Sometimes the small farmhouse design found its way into a town setting. This house was one of three nearly identical frame dwellings built next to each other in the 1860s. The addition in the rear probably housed the kitchen. The house is still standing although the entrance way has been relocated.

WASHINGTON STREET, *c.* 1909. Most of Washington Street was built by a single developer between 1908 and 1910. The majority of the houses were enlarged summer bungalows, common to the Jersey Shore. All of these residences are still standing today.

MIRROR IMAGE HOUSES, *c.* 1903. Constructed in the Queen Anne style, these two houses are identical but reversed. They are still standing on Broadway and Chandler Avenues, and have recently been restored to their original appearance.

VICTORIAN HOUSES, BROADWAY, *c.* 1880. There was no shortage of skilled carpenters in the nineteenth century, as the gingerbread on these houses can attest. Both of these houses are obscured by trees today, and much of the ornamentation has been removed. Broadway was heavily built up in the 1870s through the 1890s; many Victorian and simple frame houses were built during this time.

SUNSET VILLA, c. 1865. Built around the time of the Civil War as a residence (above), this fine Italianate-style house overlooked the Raritan Bay. In later years, it became a boarding house (left). The structure was drastically altered in an attempt to modernize it around 1910, but it gradually fell into disrepair, and by 1960 it was torn down. This type of house was also known as the "American Bracketed Villa."

Two

Stores

Isaac K. Lippincott became Keyport's first businessman after building a wood frame general store on the southwest corner of Main and Front Streets in 1831. Shortly after, in 1835, Joseph D. Hoff and Richard B. Walling built a store at 24 Front Street. Soon new and varied stores began opening. During the 1860s and '70s, each store was connected by a long wooden step and was covered by a wooden awning, protecting customers from the elements. Most of the structures were built of wood at the time, with a few brick ones scattered about. By the late 1870s businesses such as West Furniture (which is still in operation), A. Salz Furniture and Carpets, and Roberts Company began opening. By the turn of the century, over sixty stores were available to every person in town, selling clothes, medicine, housewares, and countless other items. Keyport was prospering, and soon both the Atlantic Tea Company and the Acme were operating side by side. Today, regional shopping malls have replaced the Santa Clause T Store, McKinney's Drugstore, and many others. However, many stores remain and provide a touch of charm and small town shopping that an enclosed mall can never offer.

I.K. LIPPINCOTT'S GENERAL STORE, 1830. Originally located on the corner of Front and Main Streets, this structure was moved to a lot on the north side of Front Street, near the Luppatacong Creek, around 1860. After its opening in 1832, this building became Keyport's first and only general store. After Lippincott sold out, the Walton brothers took over, and some time later one of the brothers was killed when he fell from a second-floor door. The building eventually became a private dwelling and was then converted back into a store. In its last year, it was used by N.J. Motor Sales, selling sea skiffs. The building was demolished around 1945.

RUFUS OGDEN. One of the most prominent and talented men in Keyport during the mid-nineteenth century was Rufus Ogden. Born on June 23, 1822, he opened his first business, a harness shop, in Keyport by 1850. In 1861 he was commissioned as postmaster, a position he held for over twenty-five years. By 1870, he became the first mayor of Keyport, at age forty-eight. After the Great Fire of 1877, not only did he organize the H. and L. Company, but he built the first firehouse and town hall on Broad and Third Streets. Mr. Ogden, more so than any other single person, helped to build and nurture this young town well into the twentieth century.

FERDINAND G. MAAG. Many of the photographs in this book were taken by Mr. Maag. Between 1886 and 1927, Mr. Maag captured every image possible of people, stores, families, and general scenes. He operated a studio on Front Street and resided in his home on Broadway. Mr. Maag's photography captured many of the important changes that Keyport has undergone through the years.

A VIEW OF KEYPORT, 1845. Barber and Howes' *Historical Collections of New Jersey* was one of the earliest histories of New Jersey, and also the first to contain illustrations. In this wood engraving we can see, from left to right: a steamship (possibly the *Rainbow*), the steeple of the Methodist church, the Key Port Dock, the Pavilion Hotel, and the Baptist church.

SNYDER'S ICE CREAM PARLOR, 1897. In a time before air conditioning, ice cream was a sure way to cool off in the summer heat and everyone new where to go: Snyder's. Originally located at 74 First Street (above), Snyder's moved around 1905 to a small store on Front Street. With the coming of the automobile, Snyder's took to the streets, selling homemade ice cream from large heavily-iced barrels strapped to the running boards. Snyder's remained in business until the late 1930s; the store later became Costa's Confectionery.

HUYLAR'S BICYCLE SHOP, 1890. Adam L. Huylar opened his bike shop in the old Bedle Mill around 1890. The Bedle Mill was built next to the Necius Pond outlet stream on Front and Osborn Streets in 1867. The stream and pond were later filled in and the mill became a store. Huylar's remained in business well into the 1940s, selling motorcycles, auto parts, and of course, bicycles. The building was remodeled into a furniture store but burned in 1973. The site is now a parking lot for the House of Eng Restaurant.

YE COTTAGE INN, 1920. People in the Keyport area have always craved delicious fresh seafood, and within three blocks, there were at least five seafood restaurants. The Ye Cottage Inn was opened around 1915 on Front Street near the Oyster House, by Arthur Shultze. During 1945 an attempted robbery by one of the employees led to the tragic shootings of Mr. Shultze, Ella Kurica, and Miss LaVerne Limbach. Fortunately, the victims survived, and three young men were sent to prison for the botched robbery attempt. Today, the building has been enlarged and redecorated, and people still dine there, enjoying fresh fish and steaks while overlooking the creek, marina, and bay.

COTTRELL'S RESTAURANT, 1920. Just down the street from the Ye Cottage Inn was this seafood restaurant. Located adjacent to the Matawan Creek, this business is also still in operation, under a new name. Specials of the day included the Shore Dinner, the Chicken Dinner, and the Fish Dinner, all for under $2. Other fisheries, such as Maurers, Keyport, and Burlews, all competed for the seafood business on Front Street.

A FAMILY PORTRAIT, 1890. The resemblance of these four siblings is quite apparent in this Maag photograph.

THE JOSEPH MAURER SALOON, 1880. Constructed of wood, this building was one of several that Mr. Maurer built after the 1877 fire. The building, located at the foot of Broad Street, is still standing, though it has been extensively remodeled. The wooden front porch was a fixture of all stores, and permitted travel from one store to the next, while protecting customers from the weather.

THE CONKLIN WAGON, 1900. Edwin E. Conklin operated his grocery store at 28 Front Street for many years. Originally co-owned by Edwin Beers, Mr. Conklin took over around the turn of the century. In the days before trucks, Mr. Conklin could be seen delivering his provisions with this single horse delivery wagon.

A TROLLEY WAITING ROOM, 1899. Located on First Street near Broad, this unknown store also housed the waiting room and offices of the Jersey Central Traction Company. The building was destroyed by fire during a 1960 hurricane. The well-kept lawn next door belonged to the Pavilion Hotel.

THE W.L. CONOVER SHOP, 1880. William L. Conover constructed this building and opened his harness shop here around 1878. One of the finest brick edifices in town, it was located on the south side of Front Street near Main. On Thanksgiving eve, 1889, a fire broke out in Jacob Leyrer's bakery and destroyed all the buildings in this view. Jacob Sr. was killed in the fire, and his son, Jacob Jr., died several days later from his heroic, albeit unsuccessful, attempt to rescue his father. Ironically Mr. Conover himself was a charter member of the fire department in 1877.

THE E.H. CONOVER STORE, 1875. The sign at the Conover Store on Front Street reads: "Custom and Ready Made Clothing." Built around 1860, this building has remained a retail clothing operation for nearly 140 years. Although the second floor was destroyed in a 1988 fire, the building's lines are still discernible. In the basement of the building, there are still several horse stalls and a cistern for watering the horses. This photograph is one of the earliest known images of Keyport.

RICHARD. B. WHARTON'S STORE, c. 1880. A wide array of gingerbread and decoration adorn this store in Mechanicsville. Mr. Wharton dabbled in the selling of many goods, including, pianos, organs, and sewing machines. Mail for the store could be sent to PO Box 292, or hand delivered to the store at the junction of Broad and Main Streets. South Keyport has for many years been known as Mechanicsville, because several carriage shops were located there in the 1850s. This store closed by the 1930s and at present is an apartment dwelling.

WEST FURNITURE, 1870. Robert West opened his furniture and carpet store on Front Street in 1869. It is not known where the first store stood, owing to the fact it was destroyed in the 1877 fire. One of the first furniture stores in Keyport, West Furniture is still family-owned today.

WEST FURNITURE, 1879. After his shop was destroyed by fire, Mr. West purchased the corner of First and Church for the erection of his new showroom and warehouse. Standing an impressive three-stories tall, it was one of the finest structures in town. West Furniture has always taken pride in their delivery record; from the time of horse-drawn carriages to the motorized delivery equipment of today, West still delivers fine furniture. This building was destroyed by a spectacular fire in 1976, which forced business to move a few doors away into the old post office and several other buildings. The showroom was never rebuilt and is today an empty lot.

THE CONOVER LUMBER COMPANY. First opened by Thomas S.R. Brown around 1865, this site was a lumber yard for over 120 years. Located on First Street, it was taken over by Conover's around 1927. The buildings and storage sheds were all razed in 1987 for a large condominium complex.

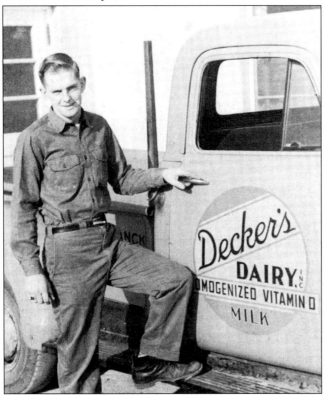

DECKER'S DAIRY. Roelof Schanck owned Decker's after graduating from high school in 1953. Decker's, which was located on Maple Place, remained in business until c. 1960. Other Keyport dairys included Paterson's Dairy on Third Street and Cosgrove's (where Golden Guernsey milk was the main product) on Second Street.

A. SALZ DRY GOODS, *c.* 1889. Mr. Salz moved into Walling Hall (above) on the corner of Front and Broad Streets around 1880. This building contained retail stores on the ground floor, and had a large assembly room and theater on the second floor, where in September 1889 one could pay 25¢ for tickets to Harriet Beecher Stowe's drama *Uncle Tom's Cabin*. Mr. Salz remained in business for many years, serving most of the local area with all types of merchandise, truly becoming the first department store in Keyport. The buildings to the right were the N.Y. and Pacific Tea Company and the American Union Tea Co. All three buildings were built in 1878. In the photograph below, a group of customers pose in front of Walling Hall around 1890. The N.Y. and Pacific Tea Co. later merged with the Atlantic and Union Tea Co. Both buildings were razed in the early 1960s.

ONE OF KEYPORT'S DINERS, 1928. Once located on the south side of Route 35, this diner served hungry shore travelers. Of course, ladies were welcome; Keyport has always been a progressive town. The diner was destroyed by fire around 1963. At one time, Keyport boasted no less than four diners: Stanley's, the Keyport, the Paramount (later the Rex), and Wilson's (later the Shore Manor).

STANLEY'S DINER, 1910–1950. Originally known as the Palace Diner, it was first managed by John Kahermanes. If one wanted a take out order, dialing 548 through the Keyport switchboard would connect you to the kitchen. Stanley's purchased the wooden diner and had a new stainless steel diner shipped in around 1950. Operated by the Conway family for many years, it was sold in the mid-1980s and is today known as the Seaport Diner. It is a classic working model of a 1950s stainless steel American diner.

Three

Industry

Industry first arrived in Keyport as early 1750, when several salt evaporating vats were erected near the Luppatacong Creek. At one time, almost all salt was made by evaporating sea water in large cast-iron caldrons. Keyport's oyster industry had its origins in 1718, when oysters were first harvested for profit. By 1840, Captain Peter Metzger planted nearly $50,000 worth of oysters in the Raritan Bay. The oyster industry arrived full scale in 1899, when the J. and J.W. Ellsworth Co. opened a huge establishment on the Luppatacong Creek. The company consisted of no less than a dozen buildings, and employed three hundred men until its demise around 1925. The Aero-Marine Plane and Motor Co. moved to Keyport in 1917, and was located on the Chingarora Creek and Raritan Bay. It landed a contract to build one third of all Army and Navy training planes; in addition, the construction of the first "passenger planes" kept workers busy until 1936. The 66-acre Aeromarine complex, when finally closed, consisted of 16 buildings, a landing field, and put over 1,600 employees out of work. The focus of Keyport today has turned primarily residential, and the many industries of long ago have given way to houses and vacant fields.

THOMAS CARHART'S CARRIAGE SHOP, 1848. Located on lower Atlantic Street, next to Carhart's Pond, this carriage shop was later purchased by Theodore Aumack. Aumack eventually sold out to Lufburrow and Walling, who built all types of carriages, wagons, and sleighs well into this century. The building was later destroyed and the pond filled in, becoming the St. John's Church parking lot.

LUFBURROW'S MILL, c. 1850. This mill was once located on Florence Avenue at the head of Chingarora Creek, directly behind Carhart's shop. The main staple of this mill was carriages and chairs. Power for the mill was harnessed from the adjacent pond, which was fed by the creek. The mill stood until about 1960.

THE TILTON AND CHERRY CARRIAGE SHOP, c. 1875. "Fine Carriages and Wagons" was the slogan of this company for many years. Located on the corner of Broad and Mott Streets, this building occupied one quarter of the entire block. Most of Keyport's early delivery wagons and fire apparatus were built in these shops. It stood until around 1916, when it was destroyed by fire. This site is now occupied by a small strip mall.

The Creek and Oyster Boats, Keyport, N. J.

AN OYSTER HOUSE AND CREEK, c. 1902. When opened in 1899, the Ellsworth Oyster Co. became one of the largest, if not the largest, producers of oysters in New Jersey. The main shucking house was located on Front Street; all oysters were brought here, opened, and then rinsed.

OYSTER WORKERS. These men clad in their leather aprons opened and cleaned hundreds of bushels of oysters per day. Each man was responsible for a segment of work, and after a long day most men and their families dined on what they cleaned all day.

OYSTER CREEK. After the large dredge boats brought in the days catch, it was unloaded onto small flat scows, and at low tide it was placed in these bushel baskets. The catch was later brought into the creek for processing. The building in this photograph became The Cove card store, and was eventually destroyed by fire—as so many other historic buildings were.

Oyster Dredge, Keyport, N. J.

AN OYSTER DREDGE. The large dredge boats would return daily with the day's harvest. Soon the oysters were transferred into smaller boats and headed into the Luppatacong Creek.

THE AEROMARINE COMPLEX, 1918. Inglis M. Uppercu moved his factory from Nutley to Keyport in 1917. Uppercu had been involved with financing the design and construction of airplanes since 1909.

THE LANDING STRIP, 1918. It was on this landing strip that many early mail planes arrived. This photograph was taken before the "Black Hanger" was constructed, which changed this view drastically. In 1987 the Keyport Historical Society and the author excavated a large piece of wing, which is now on display in the society's museum, from beneath the hanger.

THE AEROMARINE COMPLEX, 1918. Many of the structures at the Aeromarine were originally part of the old brickyard, which formally stood on this site. Many of the brickyard structures were renovated, and several new ones constructed. A large water tower was also built to provide pressure for the site. Many parts of the airport remain to this day, including the steel tie-downs for securing the airplanes in high winds.

A FLYING BOAT, 1920. This plane is possibly a model 40 flying boat. By the mid-1920s Aeromarine was turning out large flying boats such as the twelve-seat "Pinta" and "Santa Maria." These boats pioneered the development of passenger airline travel in our country.

THE INTERIOR OF A FACTORY, 1919. Here, no less than thirty navy training planes are shown under construction. When completed, these planes were shipped by train on a special spur that was built from the Central Jersey Mainline to the complex.

AN UPPERCU BUS, 1932. After the demand for planes died down, the Aeromarine complex began turning out buses. This double-decker was built in the Keyport plant; however, its final destination is unknown.

HOPLA'S COAL AND LUMBERYARD, *c.* 1924. Hopla's coal and lumberyard was located on Third Street near Waverly for many years. Coal, ice, and other home staples could be bought here. The railroad provided a spur for the delivery of coal and other larger items. The Mack truck in the background was a welcome site on cold winter days, bringing coal to basement bins everywhere in town. The site is now occupied by a condominium complex.

A BIRD'S-EYE VIEW FROM THE METHODIST CHURCH, *c.* 1889. In the center is the old Bedle Mill, still complete with its exhaust stack, which was removed around 1900. On the extreme left of the photograph is the Pavilion Hotel. Many of the long vanished East Front Street stores are shown not long after they were completed. Note the steamboats anchored at the wharf.

THE AMERICAN CUTLERY CO., *c.* 1895. This factory was originally designed to let sunlight in and increase ventilation. However, what it really did was let sunlight in, heating the factory to oven-like temperatures. The factory was occupied by Galbraiths Company for many years, which built lifeboats for the armed services and civilian ship lines. The structure still stands on Manchester Avenue.

THE KEYPORT BOTTLING COMPANY PLANT, *c.* 1912. This plant, originally operated by Elmer Morris, was located on Division Street. The Cohen family took it over around 1900 and manufactured many different types of glass containers here.

48

Four

Churches

Keyport had no organized church in the early years. All that existed was a circuit preacher, who traveled from town to town on alternate weeks teaching and inspiring local residents. By 1830 a small chapel known as St. James was erected on Broadway. It was the first of many houses of worship in Keyport, and served its Episcopal congregation until it was closed in 1849. In 1832 Nimrod and Mary Bedle held the first Methodist church service in their home. By 1841 Reverend William V. Wilson organized and built the First Baptist Church on Front Street. The Reformed Church was begun in 1845 by Reverend Millspaugh, who set about building his house of worship in 1848. St. Joseph's Roman Catholic Church was organized in 1854, near the Matawan border, and St. Mary's Episcopal Church was established by 1862. St. John's Church of Mechanicsville (officially still Raritan Township) was dedicated in 1871. In 1879 the Presbyterian congregation arrived in town, and 1892 saw the emergence of the Second Baptist Church on Atlantic Street. The Hebrew congregation met from 1860 until 1970. Today Keyport is home to other places of worship which cater equally to all beliefs, continuing the cornerstone of religion which has existed here since 1830.

THE BAPTIST CHURCH, 1860–63. In 1860 a lot was purchased on the corner of Main and Cross Streets for $500 from Beers and Walling. By 1863 mason Corneilius Ackerson had completed the building, which remained the tallest building in town for over 100 years. After 132 years, this structure is still the location of Sunday Mass.

THE FIRST BAPTIST CHURCH, 1841. William Jacques built the first Baptist church in Keyport of wood in 1841. Located on East Front Street, the edifice featured a tall steeple and six ornate stained-glass windows. It was sold to the Episcopal Church in 1863.

THE DUTCH REFORMED CHURCH, 1848. Originally located at the "Rear of the Village," it is today nearly in the center of the town. Oddly enough, the building lacked a bell tower when built.

THE FIRST PRESBYTERIAN CHURCH, 1879. This simple Gothic church was built of wood, under the direction of Reverend J.C. Elliot. The Presbyterians worshiped here until 1949, when they left the church. After sitting vacant for two years, it was bought by the Christian Science Society, who continue to occupy the building at 84 Broad Street.

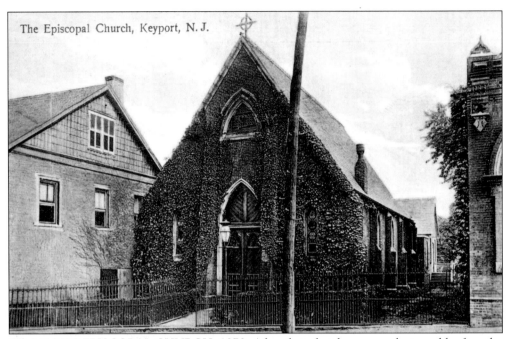

The Episcopal Church, Keyport, N. J.

ST. MARY'S EPISCOPAL CHURCH, 1878. After their first home was destroyed by fire, the congregation of St. Mary's built a fine new brick church. Located on the site of the old church on East Front Street, this edifice is still in use, minus the ivy.

INTERIOR OF ST. MARY'S EPISCOPAL CHURCH, KEYPORT, N.J.

THE INTERIOR OF ST. MARY'S. Although the church appears small from the outside, the interior is not. Graceful arches, along with a high ceiling, combine to make for a very stately interior. Note the large pipe organ to the left.

ST. JOSEPH'S ROMAN CATHOLIC CHURCH, 1879. This Gothic church was constructed after the congregation outgrew the 1854 church, and was dedicated on June 27, 1879. The spire rose 134 feet into the air, and cost $22,000 to build. In 1973, nearly one hundred summers later, the church was razed to build a new one.

THE INTERIOR OF ST. JOSEPH'S. By far the most gracious and elegant church in town, it contained no less than three alters. Above the altars was an intricate mural of the Ascension of Christ, and each side of the church was lined with stained-glass windows depicting the stations of the cross and other biblical scenes.

THE CALVARY METHODIST CHURCH, 1856. The cornerstone of this church was laid on August 5, 1856. The massive brick church was built with ornate eaves and a huge bell and clock tower. The church cost $10,000 to build, and the organ alone cost $1,000. Extensively remodeled in 1902, it is today the oldest house of worship in town.

THE CALVARY METHODIST CHURCH, 1902. With the 1902 addition the church was transformed into a medieval castle. The beautiful tower was removed and the large windows were bricked over. It was at this time that the church room itself was moved to the second floor. In 1931, a kitchen and schoolroom were added to the left side of the church.

THE INTERIOR OF THE CHURCH. In March 1952 one of the largest pipe organs in any New Jersey church was dedicated here. This church contains an elaborate amount of woodwork and is a true pleasure to worship in.

55

ST. JOHN'S METHODIST CHURCH, 1821–1895. This building (although officially in Hazlet Township) was moved from Bethany Road to the Mechanicsville section of Keyport in 1869. The small rear portion dates from 1821, while the large Victorian sanctuary was built in 1895 by Reverend Dr. O.A. Ellerson. The building was destroyed by fire in 1962, and is now the site of Remson Dodge.

THE METHODIST CHURCH, 1841. The year 1841 saw the erection of this two-story frame church next to the public school. Soon after the street was named Church Street, in honor of this edifice. It was owned by the Methodists until 1856, when it was turned over to the town. It was then used as the public school until 1871 (see p. 86).

Five

The Fire Department

The *Keyport Weekly* had warned the people of Keyport about the danger of fire for years. However, until 1877 no one seemed to be very concerned about organizing a fire department. At 11 pm on Friday, September 21, 1877, disaster struck, and by 6 am the following day over thirty-three buildings had been destroyed. On October 10, 1877, it was voted to procure a ladder truck with twenty-four leather buckets and tools, and on February 28, 1878, the Key Port Hook and Ladder Company was formally organized, with a membership of one hundred men. On August 5, 1889, the members of the Keyport Athletic Club reformed and became the Keyport Fire Company, which soon became the Keyport Engine Co. (several members of the Keyport Engine Co. would organize the Keyport First Aid Squad in 1927). The water works were built in 1893, and water flowed through the mains several months later. In March 1893 American Hose Company No. 1, which soon became the Lincoln Hose Co., was organized in Lockport. In April 1893 Raritan Hose Co. No 2 was organized by members of the Raritan Guard. In June of the same year Liberty Hose Co. No. 3 was formed in Mechanicsville. In 1907, the Brown's Point section organized Eagle Hose Co. No. 4, and in 1910 the Board of Fire Wardens, first formed in 1893, reorganized becoming their own company.

Keyport Weekly, -- Extra.

KEYPORT, N. J., SEPTEMBER 22, 1877.

KEYPORT WEEKLY.

WM. F. LeROY.

EDITOR AND PUBLISHER.

KEYPORT'S GREAT
Calamity!

Over 30 Dwellings and Business
PLACES BURNED.

The centre of the Business part of the place in ruins.

The citizens powerless, with a mass of flames extending each way from the four principal corners.

Few places have met with so heavy loss in proportion to her size, as Keyport. Many families retired Friday evening apparently as secure as they ever did, and in a few hours were houseless and homeless. With no organization, no fire department and but little water, the majority of the people worked nobly to save property, and with the timely and generous assistance of the Washington Engine Co., of Matawan, succeeded in checking the advancing flames, after about thirty dwellings, hotels, and stores were consumed.

THE FIRE

originated in the rear of A. Morris' market, in rooms of a rough wooden dwelling. The cause of its origin various reports agree in tracing to any uncertainty. The fire spread read so quickly through the building that before any organized effort could be made, it was a roaring mass of flame. Situated as it was in a row of wooden buildings, it soon became apparent that no power could save that side of the street. The occupants began to get out their goods, with volunteer help, and others started bucket lines to save the hotels on the other side, and to watch adjacent property. By great exertion the Pavilion was saved through several times on fire—and the fire part of lots occupied by Haylan's Grocery. The Mansion House, after great efforts had

were burned. On the West side of Broad, everything was burned belonging to the Walling estate, down to, and including Fred Hoffman's house, but his barn saved. Mr. Joseph Arthur and Harry Bennett, and their friend DeVeer, also did manly and noble service, both at Johnson's and at the house next east of the Episcopal church, which was saved mainly through their efforts. The Washington Fire Co., with foreman Sickles and assistant Wyckoff, with a large representation of Matawan citizens did valiant service. In fact everybody worked,—with few exceptions,—as men never worked before. It was only by almost superhuman effort that the progress of the devouring fiend was stopped. With all this noble, generous effort to save and protect our neighbors property and goods, we are deeply pained and grieved to learn that there are men so mean, so lost to all sense of human sympathy as to extend the conflagration and rob the few goods that some had been able to snatch from their burning homes. Brutes so debased, we will not honor them by calling them men—should be driven from the town.

The cry of Fire on our streets has ever been an anxious moment for us, knowing how illy we are prepared, and a lack of anything like a systematic effort to control a fire without an organization. The good people will bear us out that we have given them good counsel on this subject and urged them to take steps to prepare for just such an emergency as was predicted would happen sooner or later, and all too soon it has come in its terrible fury and our citizens have suffered an hundred fold more than would have amply equipped a complete fire department.

Will the people now come together? There will be a meeting at the WEEKLY office this evening at 8 o'clock, to organize an Aid Society, and to take such steps as will lead to a proper organization of a fire company.

APPROXIMATE LOSSES.

A. Morris,	$ 3,500
Hugh Dougherty,	2,000
Charles Miller,	2,500
Joseph Maurer,	4,500
Wolcott & Matthews,	10,000
A. Campbell, Hotel,	6,000
A. Holmes,	5,000
Ogden, Post Office,	3,500
Mansion House,	20,000
N. Johnson,	2,500
Dr. McKinney,	7,000
Episcopal Church,	3,000
John Van Woert,	1,500

Come out to the Aid Meeting to-night at the WEEKLY Office at 8 oclock.

Don't forget the Omicron Kappa Entertainment next Wednesday and Saturday evenings for the benefit of the Sufferers by the late fire. Reserved Seats for sale at McKinney's drug store.

After the fire was subdued Mr. A. Walling, Jr., made a short address censuring in just terms those miscreants who were engaged in plundering their neighbors goods and even attempting to extend the fire. He also paid a handsome compliment to those citizens who had worked so faithfully in subduing the fire. Mr. Wm. Madden followed but did not learn the tenor of his remarks.

Capt. Lee tendered the services of Company G, to do guard duty until morning.

Many cases of special service we would like to mention, but our friends will accept our thanks, and we feel all will receive the thanks of the entire community.

We take pleasure in thanking the members of Washington Fire Co., of Matawan, for their valuable aid at the fire last night.

THE *KEYPORT WEEKLY*, 1877. Printed while most of the town lay in ruin, this paper described "Keyport's Great Calamity." The *Keyport Weekly*'s office itself was heroically saved by editor and publisher William F. Leroy and his printers.

THE GREAT FIRE OF 1877. The total devastation is apparent in this view looking toward East Front Street. The photograph was taken from the white door, on the second floor (see below), of Henry H. Seabrook's store.

THE GREAT FIRE OF 1877. The Pavilion Hotel was the vantage point for this photograph, looking southwest toward Main Street. Only the basements of the Broad and Front Street stores remain. These photographs were part of a series taken of the fire's aftermath by Freehold photographer F.C. Lockwood.

THE TOWN HALL AND HOOK AND LADDER FIREHOUSE, 1885. It soon became apparent that the small frame house was not large enough to contain the town offices and the Hook and Ladder Company. Bids were advertised and work began in 1884 on the "new" town hall at the foot of East Front Street. The building contained the town commissioner's rooms, the courtroom, town offices, the jail, and room to house the ladder truck. It was dedicated in April 1886.

THE TOWN HALL AND HOOK AND LADDER FIREHOUSE, 1885. The Keyport Hook and Ladder Company was organized in 1878, at which time they took control of a Tilton and Cherry ladder truck which was already in service. By 1909, a new Seagrave ladder truck was purchased, and although it was designed to be pulled by a team of horses, KHL usually pulled the truck, uphill, BY HAND! The building ceased to be used as a firehouse in 1986, and today it is home to a store.

KEYPORT ENGINE COMPANY NO. 1. The Keyport Athletic Club reorganized as a fire company on August 5, 1889. Originally known as Keyport Fire Company No. 1, it was changed to its present name soon after. In 1890, a Holloway double-tank chemical engine was purchased and put into service at the original firehouse on First Street. The chemical engine is shown here waiting for a parade to form on the east side of Broad Street, near Front Street, around 1900.

THE ENGINE COMPANY FIREHOUSE, 1891. This fine brick and masonry station was dedicated on July 16, 1891. The building was remodeled several times, and the ornamentation was removed in the 1930s. The Main Street station was vacated in 1986, when the Engine Company and the KHL built a new combined firehouse on First Street.

LINCOLN HOSE COMPANY NO. 1, 1893. Reminiscent of the firehouses in western gold towns, this building was built on Waverly Street in 1894. The Lincoln Hose Co. was organized in March 1893, in Simeon P. Dey's cigar store on Second Street. Charter members of this company included S.P. Dey, Ezrom Walling, M.L. Terry, and several others.

LINCOLN HOSE COMPANY NO. 1. Polish your apparatus and clean and press your uniform: Inspection Day is here. Keyport's Fire Department has been annually inspected by town officials for over one hundred years. Here the Tilton and Cherry Hose Carriage of Lincoln Hose Company No. 1 is being displayed on East Front Street.

THE LINCOLN HOSE AND HOOK AND LADDER COMPANY NO. 1. After the new hook and ladder was delivered in 1909, the old one was given to Lincoln Hose Company No. 1. The company then promptly became a hose and hook and ladder company, and went about remodeling their firehouse to make room for the new equipment. By 1915 the ladder truck was disposed of, and the company became, once again, Lincoln Hose Company No. 1.

A FIRE COMPANY LIEUTENANT. This unidentified lieutenant, possibly from the Engine Company, posed for Mr. Maag around 1902.

ASSISTANT CHIEF SNYDER, 1918. Raritan Hose Company No. 2 was organized in 1893. For many years they wore unique gray coats and helmets, not only to fires, but to parades and social functions as well. Here Assistant Chief T. Walter Snyder poses in his distinct uniform. Snyder became chief of the department in 1920.

RARITAN HOSE COMPANY NO. 2, 1899. Hopefully, no one smoked around the hose carriage on this day. Heavily-decorated with straw and other flammable material, the Tilton and Cherry hose carriage of Raritan Hose Company No. 2 sits in front of the Division Street firehouse. The firehouse was moved to a lot on Broad Street in 1919, next to the Presbyterian church. It was vacated in 1969.

LIBERTY HOSE COMPANY NO. 3, 1894. On June 8, 1893, ten men met in Theodore Aumack's Carriage Factory and organized Liberty Hose Company No. 3. In the summer of 1893, a lot was procured on South Atlantic Street, and a small one-story firehouse was erected by contractor Gordon Davison. In 1894 it was decided that it was not proper to entertain ladies in the carriage room so a second story was added. The firehouse was vacated in 1948 and today is a private residence.

THE LIBERTY HOSE COMPANY, *c.* 1915. No less than eleven men are riding on this 1915 Oldsmobile, shown exiting the Atlantic Street firehouse. This truck was the first motorized fire engine in town; originally a touring car, it was rebuilt by Liberty member Alvarado Walling. It was powered by a 50-hp engine, which enabled it to win the 1916 New Jersey hose-laying competition.

A HOOK AND LADDER TRUCK, 1934. The fourth apparatus owned by the Hook and Ladder Company was delivered in 1934. Built by Diamond T, this service truck was in used until 1956. Later, after the truck failed to start, it was buried on the grounds of the Aeromarine complex.

THE 50TH ANNIVERSARY, 1927. Keyport's entire fire department turned out for its silver anniversary in 1927. A large fireman's contest, parade, and other events were organized under the direction of Chief James H. Cadoo and his assistants.

EAGLE HOSE COMPANY NO. 4, 1910. Although Brown's Point was the oldest settlement in Keyport, it was the second to last to organize a fire company. Eagle Hose Company No. 4 was organized by four men in the Disbrow Bottling Company on June 17, 1907. For many years they rented a small garage on Broadway. This firehouse, which originally housed the 1907 two-wheeled jumper shown here, today houses a 1990 Seagrave pumper which is 6 times as long and weighs about 15 more tons.

THE EAGLE HOSE ENGINE, 1961. This photograph was taken by James Atkins, a longtime photographer and former fire chief of Keyport. The sleek 1937 International was built by the Buffalo Fire Equipment Company and remained in service until 1962.

A FIRE PATROL TRUCK, 1970. The Board of Fire Wardens, commonly known as the Fire Patrol, was organized in 1910. Although the Fire Patrol originally specialized in certain activities (such as crowd control), today it operates as a complete firefighting unit, and has grown to include eighteen members.

A FIRE DEPARTMENT PORTRAIT, 1970. Every few years a new aerial photograph is taken of the fire department. From left to right are: the Fire Patrol, Eagle Hose, Liberty Hose, Raritan Hose, Lincoln Hose, the Engine Company, the Hook and Ladder, the First Aid Squad, and the Fire Chiefs. The Lincoln Hose engine is the only apparatus in this photograph still in service today.

Six

The Business District and Streets

By 1835 Keyport was beginning to take on the appearance of an actual village. Lippincott's store on Front and Main Streets was prospering. The new road to Middletown was making the deliveries to the steamboat wharf easier, and by 1833, stagecoaches began running from the Atlantic Hotel to Freehold and New Brunswick. In 1832 Leonard Walling opened his store, and in 1836 Roosevelt and Hoff began a store directly next door. During this time Keyport was planned out and many new streets were built. William Jacques completed the Pavilion Hotel in 1840, on First and Broad Streets. By 1850 the Mansion House Hotel on Broad and Front Streets was opened, and the fourth hotel in Keyport, Campbell's Railroad Hotel, opened across the street in 1860. Village mail delivery commenced in 1836, when the post office was commissioned by President Andrew Jackson. Beyond the main business district, Brown's Point had about eight stores, Mechanicsville had four, and Lockport had nearly fifteen. During the early twentieth century Keyport boasted no less than four theaters: the Palace, the Armory, the Broadway, and the Surf (later known as the Strand). Today, the oldest continuing business is Bedle's Funeral Home, which has been located in the same building since William Bedle began the business in 1841.

FRONT STREET LOOKING WEST, 1898. Many older frame structures lined the north side of Front Street until the early 1920s. The Force and Wycoff Building still stands as do both of the stores to the left of it. The trolley tracks are today covered by tons of pavement.

DOCTOR MACOMBER, 1877. Ernest P. Macomber took over Dr. Bevin's practice around 1876. His office was located above Henry Cherry's store on Front Street. He was open daily except Sundays, usually until either 8 or 9 pm. The first doctor in town was Dr. John Gregg, who settled on Broad and Front Streets in 1833.

BROAD AND FRONT STREETS LOOKING EAST, 1900. On the left is the Mansion House, a fine Keyport Hotel which was rebuilt after the 1877 fire. On the right is the Corner Drugstore, which was originally operated by Dr. McKinney. The drugstore was built in 1878 and remained open until it was razed to make way for the new Keyport Bank Building in 1928.

BROAD AND FRONT STREETS LOOKING NORTH, 1905. Saloons to the west and hotels to the east seemed to be the makeup of Broad Street at the turn of the century. Maurers and other saloons led down towards the steamboat wharf, where no less than five such establishments competed for the business of travelers. The structure with the protruding bays was built as the Llemlee Hotel in 1879. The other buildings were all built between 1877 and 1878, to replace the ones lost in the 1877 fire.

EAST FRONT STREET, 1901. All of the stores on the north side of East Front Street (left) were built between 1877 and 1885. They remained until the early 1970s, when they were removed because of "Urban Blight." The land remained empty until 1987, when an office complex was built on the site.

EAST FRONT STREET, 1951. By the 1950s East Front Street was beginning to show its age. The cigar store in the above photograph is now the Army and Navy surplus store; Alpine's Department Store is a few doors down, but it later moved and remained open until the owners retired in the 1980s.

THE PETER P. CONOVER HOUSE, 1863. This fine Greek Revival dwelling was built on land originally owned by Issac Lippincott. In later years, the house was remodeled and surrounded by stores. Today it is barely recognizable and still stands wedged in between the Borough Hall and stores.

THE BROWN BLOCK, 1927. The Brown Printing and Publishing Company moved their offices here from across the street in 1927. The *Keyport Weekly* and *Matawan Journal* were printed here until the company's demise in 1972. Note the Conover House in the background. The building today houses several commercial establishments.

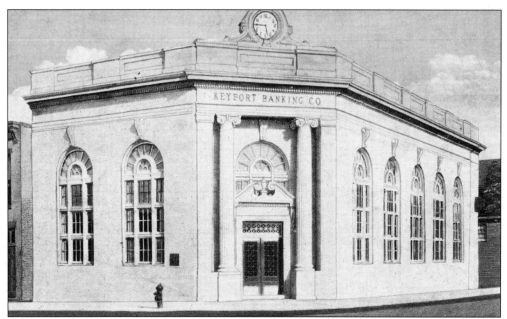

THE KEYPORT BANKING COMPANY, 1928. This fine bank building was built under the direction of President F. Palmer Armstrong. It replaced an earlier building on Front Street which was built in 1884. The new building was built on the site of McKinney's Drugstore (see p. 71). It still stands today, but is under new management.

THE PEOPLE'S NATIONAL BANK, 1923. Opened on 25 Front Street, this structure replaced an earlier bank built in 1890 on Broad Street. Although the large windows have been covered over, it is still open today as the United Jersey Bank.

THE WASHINGTON HOTEL, 1850. This hotel and the adjoining feed store were built at 470 Main Street around 1850. It was located in Mechanicsville and overlooked Carhart's Mill Pond, which is now the St. John's Church parking lot. The hotel still stands and is now an apartment building.

FIRST STREET LOOKING EAST, 1900. On the right is the Gallagher House, one of the largest Victorian houses in Keyport. It was built between 1880 and 1882 on the corner of First and Atlantic Streets. It was later dubbed the Mansion House, and continues as an apartment building under that same name today. Many Victorian houses, with their towers and widow watches, grace First Street along the bay.

THE PAVILION HOTEL, 1840. William Jacques constructed the finest Keyport hotel on the corner of First and Broad Streets in 1840. The building originally contained over eighty guest rooms, a saloon, and a laundry. It was frequented for many years by the multitudes of travelers that came through the port. Although partially destroyed by fire in 1851, it was rebuilt, and in 1877 again narrowly escaped destruction by fire.

THE PAVILION HOTEL. For many years bands would gather on the massive front porch, and people would come to hear them play and to relax on the fine lawn overlooking the bay. In 1913, the hotel was remodeled and renamed the Raritan Inn. The third floor was destroyed by fire in 1932 and rebuilt. This historic structure remained a hotel until 1957, when it closed for good. Finally, on April 25, 1962, the building was completely destroyed in the largest Keyport fire since 1877. The lot is now the home of an office complex built in 1987.

THE NORTH SIDE OF FRONT STREET, 1925. Since 1925 several new stores have been built on the left. In 1923 Hopkins Drugs was built to resemble the Bank, albeit on a smaller scale. The Bogardus Building was built in 1906 and became J.J. Newberry's 5 and 10 around 1940. Newberry's is still open for business, but the "5 and 10" has been taken off the facade.

FRONT STREET LOOKING EAST, 1908. Some of the finest houses in town were built on Front Street, between Main and Beers Streets. Among them were these Greek Revival dwellings: the Column House (built c. 1837 by F. Decker); the Captain C.D. Emson House (c. 1860); and the Captain G.W. Johnson House (c. 1847). The Column House included a two-story open portico which was common to southern plantation houses.

FRONT STREET, 1951. Keyport has always enjoyed elements of small town America. In this photograph the streets are lined with busy stores and long-gone diagonal parking spaces, while on the left a police officer talks on the callbox. Keyport's Police Department was formed in the early 1920s. One of the first patrolmen was Asbury "Ash" Mount. Up to that time law and order consisted of a town constable, supplemented by the New Jersey State Police. During the 1950s the police station was located in a storefront on Broad Street. It remained at this location until the J.C.P. & L. Building on Main Street was purchased to be the borough hall and police station, c. 1953.

A MAAG PORTRAIT, *c.* 1905. This young man posed with his hat and cane for Ferdinand Maag in Maag's Front Street studio.

BROAD STREET, 1920. The Raritan Hose Company finished moving their firehouse next to the Presbyterian church in 1919; a short time later, the Keyport Central Garage opened on the corner of Third and Broad Streets.

ATLANTIC STREET LOOKING SOUTH, 1900. Thomas S.R. Brown opened his lumber company on the corner of Atlantic and First Streets around 1865. During the nineteenth and twentieth century the Conover Lumber Company constructed two mill complexes: one on Division Street near the railroad, and the other on Atlantic Street. The building in the foreground was originally A. Bedle's Shoe Store. The First Street yard housed the showroom, hardware store, and main lumberyard. The lumber company was razed in 1987 (see p. 36).

Main and Front Sts., Keyport, N. J.

MAIN STREET LOOKING SOUTH. A lone horseless carriage is traveling north, soon to pass the Engine House and enter the business district for some summer shopping. Note the early wooden street signs. This view was radically changed with the building of the Brown Block in 1928. Keyport's streets remained unpaved until the 1920s, when they were first cemented.

Broadway, Keyport N. J. looking west.

BROADWAY LOOKING WEST, 1910. In this photograph a Jersey Central Traction Company trolley starts to round the Front Street corner, while a few young boys sneak into the picture. During this time the trolley car barn was located in Union Beach, about 1.5 miles from this location.

Broadway, Looking North, Keyport, N. J.

BROADWAY LOOKING NORTH, 1919. As we pass the Eagle Hose firehouse on the right, we come to the Broadway Meat Market—and maybe pick up some steaks and chopped beef for dinner. Perhaps we should fuel our Model T Ford at the corner gas pump before heading home . . .

THE FIVE CORNERS, 1928. The five corners once existed at the intersection of Broadway, Maple Place, and Highway 35. It was later rerouted by an overpass and several jughandles. The large building on the right was originally the car barn for the Keyport and Matawan Street Railway. It was owned by the Aeromarine Corporation when it was destroyed by fire in 1920, at a loss of $60,000.

THE MANSION HOUSE, 1878. The second Mansion House was completed in 1878, to replace the one that burned in the 1877 fire. Its five-sided design was unusual for the time. It remained a hotel until *c.* 1928, when it was remodeled into its present use: stores and apartments.

Surf Theatre and Front St.,
Keyport N. J.

THE SURF THEATER, *c.* 1906. Keyport's most palatial theater stayed open for nearly eighty years. At first it showed silent films, but soon talking films hit the big screen. A marquis was added in the 1930s and it became a XXX adult theater in the 1970s. During the 1980s the marquis was removed and it was remodeled into commercial space. It today houses a coffee shop with a fine view of the Raritan Bay.

THE MOTT STREET BRIDGE, 1898. For many years Mott Street ended at Luppattacong Creek. In 1898 the town commissioners voted to erect this steel bridge over the creek. The bridge carried traffic until the late 1950s, when the creek was routed through a culvert and the bridge was dismantled.

Seven

Schools

The Key Port Company donated land for the first school in 1835. Within a year the "little red schoolhouse" was built and in use on the corner of Church and John (Second) Streets. This building served Keyport children until 1856, when the schoolhouse was replaced by the Methodist church house located next door. Professor George W. Holmes conducted classes from 1862 until about 1890 in Agricultural Hall at the corner of Front and Church Streets. By 1871 the population of Keyport had reached nearly 2,000 people, and it was evident that a new school was needed, so the Board of Trustees purchased the lot bounded by Broad, Elizabeth, Division, and Mott (Maple Place) Streets, for the erection of the new Graded School. New schools were built in Lockport in 1904 and Brown's Point in 1907. In 1928 the Keyport children of grades nine through twelve received a new high school, built on South Broad Street. In 1960 the Keyport Central School was built to release some of the burden from the then overcrowded classrooms at the Graded School. By 1966 the Graded School was becoming unsafe and it was finally condemned and razed in 1967, after serving the village for nearly one hundred years.

THE PUBLIC SCHOOL, 1835. The "little red schoolhouse," as it was known, was located on Church Street for many years. It ceased being a school in 1856. It was later moved to the Bay View House property on First Street, where it became a laundry house. By the time this photograph was taken the building was abandoned and long forgotten. It was razed sometime around 1935.

THE PUBLIC SCHOOL, 1856. Located on the corner of Church and John (Second) Streets, this building replaced the 1835 structure. Originally constructed as the Methodist church, it was sold to the school district in 1856. During this time the stained-glass windows were removed, as was the bell tower. It served as a school until 1871, and remained standing until the mid-1960s, when it was razed. The 1841 brownstone foundation can still be traced.

SCHOOLGIRLS, 1900. This group of schoolgirls includes many local names such as Hobart, Walling, Ogden, and Morris. The location of the photograph has been lost to obscurity; however, it may have been Wheeler's Academy, which was once located on Broad Street.

A YOUNG GIRL, 1895. This unidentified young girl was photographed by Maag in 1895. Her style of dress could be categorized as "popular Victorian."

THE GRADED SCHOOL, 1871–78/1912. Keyport schoolchildren attended school in this building on Mott (Maple Place) Street for ninety-five years. Corneilus Brown was the mason and the carpentry work was completed by James H. Johnson. The school was built of brick and cost $26,000 to complete. The high school addition was finished in 1878, at which time it doubled the size of the school. School bells' hung in both the north and south towers until 1909.

THE GRADED SCHOOL. The school was remodeled in 1912 with the addition of larger windows, new classrooms, and a gymnasium. Baseboard heat was installed that year, replacing the many coal stoves that heated each classroom. By the 1930s the belltowers were removed and all of the trees were cut down. Throughout the years the school has been known as the Graded School, the Grammar School, and the Broad Street School. This historic structure was closed in 1965–66 and razed in 1967. The site is occupied today by a 7-11 store and several houses.

STUDENTS OF THE GRADED SCHOOL, 1890. The teacher was Drusilla Matthews, the place was Broad Street, and the year was 1890: these fourth grade students are shown posing for an annual class picture, which was taken outside until the 1940s.

GRADED SCHOOL STUDENTS, 1905. "Boys to the left, girls to the right" may have been the call for this class photograph on a fall day at the old Grammar School. Note the Gothic arched window (far right) and the intricate brick paving, which once surrounded the entire school building.

THE EAST KEYPORT SCHOOL, 1904–1927. This fine school was built on Second Street in the Lockport section of town. It was approved by the newly formed Board of Education, which replaced the Board of Trustees in 1901. In 1927 the building was completely altered, and the school was doubled in size. The school still stands, and today serves as the regional senior citizens center.

EAST KEYPORT STUDENTS, 1910. Both classrooms turned out for this photograph by Maag in 1910. The small windows flanking the entrance were where the restrooms were located. All of the children from Lockport attended this school until it was consolidated with the Central School in 1984–85.

West Keyport School, Keyport, N. J.

THE WEST KEYPORT SCHOOL, 1907. Once located on Washington Street, this school was a familiar site for over eighty years. Children from Brown's Point attended this classic turn-of-the-century structure until 1984. It was abandoned and, sadly, destroyed by fire in 1988. The site is today occupied by several houses.

THE KEYPORT HIGH SCHOOL, 1928. The Class of 1929 was the first class to graduate from the new high school. The beige brick building is located on South Broad Street and includes several fine sculptures in the brickwork. Architecturally, this building could be classified as the "Educational Renaissance-style." The school's main entrance includes fine ceramic tile walls and a large chandelier suspended from the ceiling. Additional classrooms were built in 1938 and 1955. In 1966 the old gymnasium/auditorium was rebuilt into classrooms, and a new gym was built on the Monroe Street side.

THE KEYPORT HIGH BAND, 1968. Even a small school was capable of having an orchestra-sized musical ensemble. The Keyport Band was for many years one of the largest and finest in the northern shore area. Band Director Homer Gurlufsen later became principal of the Central School and retired around 1983. The band was a staple at the many Keyport vs. Matawan games that took place on Thanksgiving on the school's athletic field. The field, built in 1937–38 by the Works Project Administration, is still located at the end of Jackson Street.

H. STANLEY "TUFFY" BAKER. Tuffy, as he was known to thousands of Keyport High School students, taught physical education and driver's education from 1948 to 1980, when he retired as athletic director. In addition to being the head football coach and leading Keyport to many gridiron victories, Tuffy was a basketball, baseball, and track coach. When he wasn't teaching or coaching he worked as a "barber" in several Keyport shops, with other barbers such as William "Smokey" Shumock, Al Hoffman, and Larry Vecchio.

THE VARSITY FOOTBALL TEAM, 1979. Here the varsity gridiron team is posed for the 1979 team photo. Coached by Mike Ciccotelli (front center) and John Dumford (left rear), the team consisted of players such as Former Keyport Mayor John Merla (top row, third from right), Keyport Police Officer Anthony Gallo (second row, far left), and area contractor Steve Svensen (next to Gallo). Today Assistant Coach Dumford has moved to superintendent of the Keyport school system after starting as a guidance counselor in 1976. "Chic" is still coach, leading the team to more victories under his leadership than any other in Keyport history.

94

Eight
The Bay and Her Boats

Keyport's prosperity in the eighteenth and nineteenth centuries can be directly attributed to the fine location it holds on several waterways. The most important of these is the Raritan Bay, which links Keyport and Monmouth County to New York City's wharves by a mere 22 miles. By 1725 Thomas Kearny had taken advantage of Keyport's position and established a trade route from his home on Luppattacong Creek to Manhattan Island, running sloops several times a month. In 1835 Roosevelt and Hoff established a yard at the foot of Church Street on the bay, but the first ship built in Keyport was completed around 1839 in the yards of John Cottrell in Brown's Point. By 1849 Benjamin Terry moved his shipbuilding business from New York City to the mouth of the Luppattacong Creek. Such ships as the *Keyport* (1853), the *Jesse Hoyt* (1862), and the *River Queen* (1864) plied the waters of the Raritan Bay. Terry moved his yard around 1860 to the foot of Myrtle Avenue in Lockport, where shipbuilding continued on a smaller scale well into the twentieth century. Since 1900 other boat builders have taken up shop in this bayside village. Today such names as Olav Olsen and Hans Pedersen and Sons all contribute to shipbuilding and marina business on the Raritan Bay.

The STEAMBOAT DOCK, KEY PORT, 1830–31. The Key Port Company built this dock and storehouse in 1830 at the foot of Broad Street. The sloops *New Jersey* and *Middletown* were the first to sail from Keyport to New York City in 1830. In 1839 Captain Chumar was operating the *Monmouth* with a 12.5¢ fare for round trip excursion from Keyport to New York. The Key Port Company dissolved in 1839 and sold the dock and the sloops. By 1851 the Key Port Dock Company was begun; they rebuilt the wharf, and the 275-foot steamer *Reindeer* was placed in service.

THE STEAMBOAT *KEY PORT*, 1853. In this painting by James Bard, the *Key Port* is depicted in full sail on the Raritan bay. She was built by Benjamin Terry in his Keyport yard and was one of the finest vessels ever to sail out of town. The *Key Port* was 175 feet long and nearly 365 tons. She ceased running in Keyport in 1862 and her name was changed to the *James T. Brett*. During the war she was operated by the U.S. Army Quartermaster detachment, shuttling troops on the Potomac River. She was finally scrapped in 1918.

STEAMBOAT DOCKS, *c.* 1880. On November 20, 1862, the Key Port and Middletown Steamboat Company was formed. This new company replaced the Key Port Dock Company as the sole operator of the Key Port wharf. The Key Port Dock was expanded around 1865 with the addition of the Holmdel Dock to the east. This dock was built for the steamboat *Holmdel,* and both docks remained until the 1940s, when they were destroyed by hurricanes.

THE STEAMBOAT *HOLMDEL, c.* 1870. The steamboat *Holmdel* was built in 1865, and was commanded by Captain John S. Conover for many years. Named after the township where most of her produce was grown, she ran between Keyport and New York City until around 1905, when she was cut up for scrap.

AN UNKNOWN CAPTAIN, c. 1879. This man has definitely been identified as a Keyport boat captain, but further identification has proven difficult. It is possible that he is Captain V.R. Woodward, who commanded the steamer *Minnie Cornell* in the 1880s. The *Minnie Cornell* was 183 feet in length and was in operation from 1879 until 1893.

BOATS AT THE YACHT CLUB, c. 1915. The Key Port Boat Club was organized in 1908 by the following men: Henry Toft, Harry Coons, William Gills, and Thomas and Richard Burrowes. In 1909 the name was changed to the Key Port Yacht Club, and in the years that followed many sailboat regattas were held, as well as fish suppers and social fundraisers. In 1923 the Yacht Club merged with the Keyport Social Club, to double the Yacht Club's membership. The club has had its dock destroyed by hurricanes, and in 1981 its clubhouse was destroyed by fire; it has always rebuilt, however, and today it remains a premier yachting club of the Jersey Shore.

THE STEAMBOAT *KEY PORT II*, *c.* 1871. The *Key Port II* is often confused with the first. Although she never plied from Keyport, she did spend her winters berthed at the steamboat dock. She was operated by the Keansburg Steamboat Co. and sank in 1917, in New York's East River. Ironically, the two ships were both scrapped in 1918. The *Key Port II* was originally built as the *Martha's Vineyard* in New York City.

THE MUNICIPAL FISHING PIER, 1960. Crabbing has always been both a sport and a small profit for many people along the Raritan Bay and her creeks. Here a mother and her children crab off the old fishing pier, which was replaced in 1976 with a new pier.

MATAWAN CREEK. This creek separates Keyport from the Township of Aberdeen. Originally large sloops plied the waters towards Matawan, but by 1840 the bottom became filled with silt and Keyport took over the shipping trade. The first crossing here was a ferry operated by John Kuhns in 1854. After many years of debate a wooden toll bridge was built in 1857, and in 1888 it was replaced by an iron bridge. Since 1915 at least three other bridges have been built at this location.

THE WATERFRONT, 1889. This view shows the beach and houses along First Street. At one time most homeowners had small docks and carriage houses which extended into the bay on pilings. The Chingarora Dock (to the left) was built in 1846 to compete with Key Port Dock, which was about three blocks down on First Street. The Chingarora Dock was owned by the Chingarora Dock Company, who operated the sloop *Golden Rule*. The dock was later owned by the Brown Lumber Company, and was dismantled by 1920.

THE RARITAN BAY. The Raritan Bay has been home to many different types of water activities, both commercial and pleasure. Many years of neglect and pollution have been reversed in the last decade and the bay has returned to her former splendor. It is even rumored that slowly the oyster/clamming population is returning.

THE *CITY OF NEW YORK*, *c.* 1912. The *City of New York* was operated by the Keansburg Steamboat Co. until about 1949. She made daily excursion trips to New York and was berthed in the winter at the old Key Port Dock. She was originally built in 1912 in Sparrows Point, Maryland. The hurricane of 1950 caused her to be released from her winter mooring at Key Port, were she became beached and was soon cut up for scrap.

THE BEACHFRONT NEAR LOCKPORT, *c.* 1890. All along the bay small and large vessels were built on the beach. Here a two-masted schooner is nearing completion at the Terry Yard, near the Bay View House property. Fishing nets were a common site along the beachfront; laid to dry and mended daily, the fishermen's nets were the most important part of his livelihood, next to his boat.

THE BAY AND RAILROAD PIER, *c.* 1899. The great pier of the New York and Freehold Railroad was completed in 1880. Trains which took the First Street spur boarded passengers and freight at the terminus of this nearly 2,000-foot-long pier. It was closed by 1890 and burned in 1915.

ALONG THE WATERFRONT, *c.* 1905. Keyport's waterfront has changed little in the past one hundred years. New docks have replaced old ones and boats of all types are still anchored in the natural harbor, which Keyport has always utilized to its best extent.

THE FRONT STREET BRIDGE, *c.* 1908. The Luppattacong Creek Bridge was first built around 1840. Until that time the creek had to be forded at low tide. Here the second bridge is shown, which was built about 1875 and replaced in 1910. The bridge was damaged by a fire in a boat in 1988, and today has a load restriction an attempt to increase its lifespan.

FIRST STREET HOUSES IN A STORM, *c.* 1905. Winter northeasters visit with destructive force on occasion. Here the rear of houses along First Street are being battered by the storm's fury. This photograph was taken from the end of a long vanished dock at 37 First Street. Note the bathhouses on the left and the roof of the Armory in the background. The small frame house served as the first firehouse for the Keyport Engine Co. from 1889 to 1891.

THE BEACHFRONT AND THE TERRY SHIPYARD, *c.* 1900. Here another large steamboat is being constructed by the Terry Yard at the foot of Myrtle Avenue. Terry moved his yard to Keyport in 1853 and relocated from Brown's Point to Lockport around 1865. Much of the old marine railway and launch are still intact and can be found at low tide along the beach.

BOATS AND STEAMBOATS, 1908. Several small skiffs are in the foreground, while two steamboats are at the wharf. The location is the beach behind 100 First Street.

OYSTER CREEK, c. 1900. The Luppattacong Creek has been nicknamed Oyster Creek since the turn of the century. The creek led to the Key Grove Farm, which was the destination of the first sailing vessels in the area.

THE REMAINS OF THE STEAMBOAT DOCK, 1969. Encased in ice, these jagged reminders of Keyport's past are the remains of the steamboat dock. Ravaged by hurricanes, the last parts of the dock were destroyed in 1960. Today only a fraction of the pilings remain; soon nearly two hundred years will have passed since they were first driven into the sand by the men of the Key Port Company in 1830.

Nine

Recreation

There was little time for leisure in the lives of Keyporters in eighteenth and nineteenth centuries. Long days of working the pound nets, repairing nets, clamming, and building new vessels took up much time. Women and children also spent their days cleaning and taking care of the household. When holidays did come they were welcomed, and much preparation was made to make the fullest use of all free time. In the 1850s nearby Cliffwood became a popular bathing and water recreation spot. Located nearby in Matawan (Aberdeen) Township, Cliffwood was a vast expanse of sandy beaches and peaceful woodlands. By the 1920s Cliffwood was being heavily developed by the firm of Morrisey and Walker. Streets were laid out, hundreds of summer bungalows were built, and a beautiful boardwalk with amusements was constructed. The boardwalk was destroyed in the 1940s by repeated hurricanes. Keyport's Pavilion Beach was opened around 1905, and catered to boaters and bathers. The Salt Water Festival was begun in the late nineteenth century; featuring baby and firemen's parades, contests, block parties, and dances, it later evolved into Keyport Day, which continued into the 1960s.

THE 1908 KEYPORT CARNIVAL. It seems the entire town has turned out for this parade as it heads north on Main Street. The local constabulary is in place for some traffic direction, and to keep young children and those who tipped a few to many in place during the festivities.

OTHER VIEWS OF THE 1908 KEYPORT CARNIVAL. Who will be the winner of the baby parade? Only the judges know for sure. Here the proud Victorian mothers head toward the viewing stand with the ornate carriages and the soon-to-be prizewinners.

THE KEYPORT BRASS BAND, c. 1902. These band members pose in front of the Armory building on First Street. Instruments of the day included the baritone horn, coronets, a snare drum, and, of course, a bass drum. The band was organized about 1880 and continued until about 1920. By the time the bottom photograph was taken the band appears to have doubled in size.

A YOUNG BOY ON A WHEEL. Many older residents often referred to bicycles as a "wheel." This young man seems to be enjoying his high seat on this old cycle, and should be thanking the front porch for an act that would have been impossible.

Seeing Keyport, N. J.

Copyrighted 1907, by Tichnor Bros., Inc.
Pat. applied 1or.

A KEYPORT POSTCARD, c. 1909. This postcard, when opened, contained twelve interesting views of Keyport. It is doubtful that the ungainly vehicle on the card ever saw service in Keyport; however, the load of tourists ready to see the sights around the village was an accurate depiction.

THE CLIFFWOOD HOUSE, c. 1865. Located on a bluff overlooking the bay, this three-story hotel was built by Dr. Kent in 1850. This sketch was made by George Birch Jr. from memory in 1920. George Birch Sr. operated a nearby picnic grove near Treasure Lake until the 1880s. The Cliffwood House was destroyed by fire between 1875 and 1880.

SIEDLERS BEACH, c. 1910. Siedlers was located on Cliffwood Beach, north of Whale Creek. An early entertainment center, bathing, boating, and "good eatin" were to be had at this resort on the bay. The area closed during the 1940s and burned to the ground soon after. Today it is an area of quiet beach grass and sandy dunes.

THE CLIFFWOOD POOL, *c.* 1928. The Sportland pool was located at the terminus of the Cliffwood Boardwalk. It was built around 1920 and was one of the finest salt water pools on the shore. The pool was closed in the 1960s and later abandoned. Today the pool's light blue cement edge is still visible emerging from beneath the sand and cattails.

Bathing at Belleview Beach near Key Port. N. J.

THE BELLEVIEW BATHING BEACH, *c.* 1912. These bathers appear to be practicing gymnastics at the Belleview Beach, which is thought to have been located east of Keyport.

113

THE 90th ANNIVERSARY OF THE FIRE DEPARTMENT, 1967. Saturday, October 4, 1967, was the date of the 90th anniversary celebration of the Keyport Fire Department. Here the department, led by Fire Chief Frank "Junior" Vanpelt and assistants Don Redmond and Howard Creed, march through the same street where ninety years ago people stood homeless from the fire of 1877.

THE HIGH SCHOOL BAND, c. 1951. Keyport's High School's band is seen here crossing Broad Street on Front, while leading a victory parade. Led by several twirlers and the drum majorette, Keyport's band always marched after a victorious football game.

114

CARHART'S POND, 1911. Located on Florence Avenue in Raritan Township, this pond was filled in around 1960. In its time it was well-known for the boating, fishing, and ice skating that it offered.

A CARNIVAL FLOAT, c. 1903. The first flag is portrayed, with a young Betsy Ross at the spinning wheel, in this annual Fourth of July parade. This view looks towards the Force and Wycoff Building on Front Street near Broad.

THE WEST FURNITURE FLOAT, *c.* 1905. Even local business entered floats into the carnival parades. It was a great advertisement at that time; however, furniture deliveries had to wait until the parade was over.

THE PAVILION BEACH. A large tent has been put up on the property, possibly for the Salt Water Day celebration in 1906. The park at the time extended from the lawn of the Pavilion Hotel, across First Street, and terminated at the Raritan Bay. The property is today known as Beach Park and is home to the municipal boat ramp.

Ten

All Around the Town

From the beginning getting to and from places was an important part of life. Steamboats, stagecoaches, trains, trolleys, and automobiles each had tremendous impacts on the lives of the people of Keyport. Steamboats arrived in 1830 and offered a new method of travel to the town. The first stagecoaches were begun from both the Atlantic Hotel and the Pavilion Hotel by 1840. With the beginning of stagecoaches several toll roads were constructed. Tolls were collected for the maintenance of the roads (usually planks and cinders) and the salaries of the toll collectors. The railroad was chartered as early as 1848 but it did not materialize until 1870, eventually becoming the Freehold and New York Railroad in 1871. It is unknown where the first railroad platform stood, but in 1890 a new brick station was built at the corner of Broad and Butler Streets by the Central Railroad of New Jersey. In May 1887 the first street railway was constructed. The Keyport and Matawan Street Railway operated until 1901, when it became electrified. It then became the Jersey Central Traction Company until its demise in 1923. Soon buses took the place of trolleys and used the same routes, many of which still continue to be used to this day.

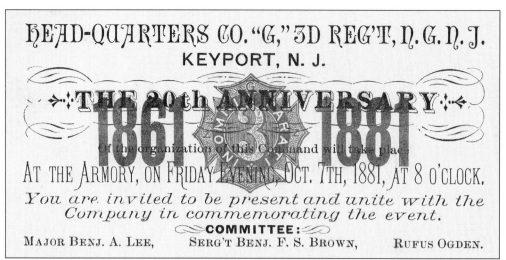

HEAD-QUARTERS CO. "G," 3D REG'T, N.G.N.J.

KEYPORT, N. J.

THE 20th ANNIVERSARY

1861 3 1881

of the organization of this Command will take place

AT THE ARMORY, ON FRIDAY EVENING, OCT. 7TH, 1881, AT 8 O'CLOCK.

You are invited to be present and unite with the Company in commemorating the event.

COMMITTEE:

MAJOR BENJ. A. LEE,   SERG'T BENJ. F. S. BROWN,   RUFUS OGDEN.

AN ARMORY ANNIVERSARY TICKET, c. 1881. The Keyport unit of the New Jersey National Guard was formed in 1861, and fought for the 29th N.J. Volunteers in the Civil War. This ticket was issued for their 20th anniversary in 1881.

THE KEYPORT NATIONAL GUARD ARMORY, 1909. Here the National Guard Armory is shown after being partially destroyed by a suspicious fire in 1909. The fire destroyed the library on the second floor and much of the assembly hall. The Armory was built in 1879, and stood at 40 First Street, where it replaced the Uriah Dudley Canning Factory, which burned in 1877. This building was also the first home of the Raritan Hose Co., which occupied the area behind the doors to the right of the photograph from 1893 until 1900. After the fire the Armory became a theater, until it was abandoned in the late 1960s. It collapsed in 1973. The site is today occupied by the consolidated firehouse of the Hook & Ladder and Engine Co.

A TOLLHOUSE, c. 1880. Tell Roberts seems to be taking a nap at the tollhouse on South Atlantic Street. The structure stood opposite of Carhart's Pond and charged tolls for every wagon, carriage, and sled that entered Winkletown (another term for South Keyport) in the last half of the nineteenth century. Note the stovepipe in the rear for those blustery winter days. The building in the background is part of a feed and grain store that was once connected to the Washington Hotel (see p. 79).

THE KEYPORT STATION OF THE CENTRAL RAILROAD OF NEW JERSEY, 1890. This one-and-a-half-story brick structure with hipped roof and flared eaves was a classic example of Queen Anne architecture adapted to a small town station. Built to replace an earlier wooden platform, this station was located on the corner of Broad and Butler Streets. It remained a regular stop until the 1950s, when passenger service was discontinued. At one time this was one of three passenger stations in town. The second station was located on First Street at Sylvanus and Benjamin Lee's store. The third was located at the terminus of the great pier. The station was abandoned around 1960 and stood until it was destroyed by a suspicious fire on July 4, 1966. The site is now a small park.

THE RARITAN GUARD LIBRARY, 1912–13. After the small library in the Armory was destroyed a new location was needed. In 1912 a lot was purchased on the corner of Broad and Cross (Third) Streets were a fine two-story library was constructed. The building was later taken over by the Keyport Library Association, and is today operated as a division of the Keyport government by a board of trustees. The library has itself just recently been landscaped and brought up to current standards.

A MEMORIAL TABLET, 1919. Erected in honor of those who served in the Civil War, the Spanish-American War, and World War I, this monument was made possible by the ladies auxiliary of the library, generous donations, and a cash gift from the mayor and council. Since this monument was dedicated, others have been erected for those who served in World War II, Korea, and Vietnam. Sadly, many of Keyport's young men never returned to their hometown, to their true loves, and to their families because of these conflicts.

THE WATER WORKS, 1893.
Located at the foot of Cedar Street,
the first pumping station was built in
1893. Soon indoor plumbing
replaced outhouses and made life on
cold winter mornings, both in the
kitchen and the bathroom. This
station was constructed of brick and
was powered by steam. Several wells
over 100 feet deep drew water from
the underground aquafier into the
filters of the station. It was replaced
in 1923–24.

FRANK "ZIPPY" WALLING,
c. 1950. Mr. Walling was the
operator of the Water Works for
many years. He never failed to wear
his suit and tie to work with his
accompanying black derby. "Zippy"
was also a longtime member of the
Liberty Hose Co. He resided on
Broad Street near Warren.

THE NEW WATER WORKS, 1923. Built to replace the 1893 station, this fine building was finished with very bright yellow bricks and gilded with dark green trim. Powered by electricity, this station was a engineering marvel in its day. Many a thirsty lad may remember its ice cold water fountain, which was a savior after playing on those hot days in Wiegand's Woods. It was replaced in 1985 and razed in 1986. It is now the site of the Benjamin Terry Park.

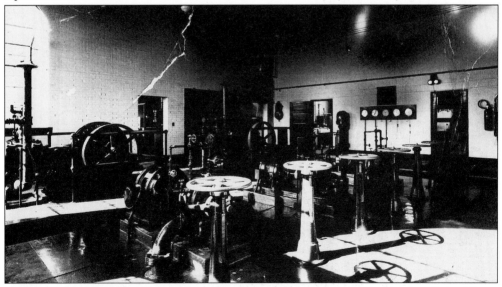

THE INTERIOR OF THE WATER WORKS. The process of water filtration has changed very little in the past one hundred years. Water is pumped into the treatment plant and filtered with charcoal and lime; chlorine is then added, while bacteria and Ph levels are checked. It is then pumped into a holding tank where it is ready to use.

J.C.T. COMPANY CONDUCTORS, *c.* 1910. Claude Evans (left) worked for the traction company from the days of the horse cars until the company ceased operations in 1923. Around 1912 Mr. Evans was witness to a murder on a trolley, when a man boarded the trolley and gunned the motorman down.

THE LAST HORSE CAR, 1901. These two large steeds would soon be auctioned off, for they were replaced by electricity. This photograph was taken in front of the old car barn on lower Broadway.

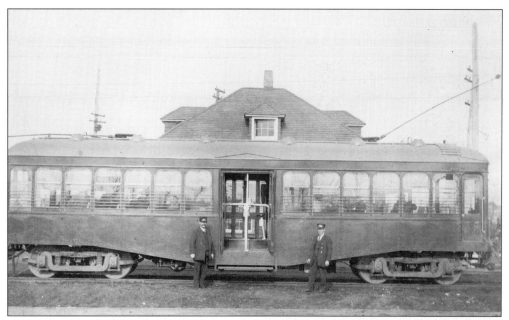

A STEEL CENTER DOOR TROLLEY, 1915. This new steel trolley was placed in service on June 28, 1915. It is shown here at the Campbell's Junction stop in Middletown. Originally the trolley line of the J.C.T. Co. ran through Freehold, Matawan, Keyport, Keansburg, and Campbell's Junction to points south.

CAR NO. 2 OF THE J.C.T. CO., *c.* 1908. The most common type of trolley operated by the company was the Brill or St. Louis Manufacturing Company's end door trolley. Conductors were proud of their cars and often posed with them. Note the cow catcher on the front: although not many cows roamed the area, it was useful in moving an occasional stubborn mule or horse.

THE POWERHOUSE, 1902. Located on Florence Avenue in Union, this building provided power for the trolley's overhead cantilever wiring system. Union became Union Beach after it was developed in the 1920s. The powerhouse is currently used by the Jersey Central Power and Light Company (the heirs of the J.C.T) as a storage area, minus the stack and the building on the left.

A CARRIAGE AT MECHANICSVILLE, 1885. This small stagecoach was originally known as an omnibus. It was built in Aumack's Carriage Shop, and though it did not see service in Keyport, many of its builders and several townspeople gathered for its completion.

THE FIRE DEPARTMENT DRUM AND BUGLE CORP, 1949. The Keyport Fire Department was at one time accompanied to all large parades by this band. This photograph was taken at the athletic field, on the football bleachers.

ELIZABETH STRONG, 1865. A distant relative of *Keyport Weekly* publisher J. Mabel Brown, Ms. Strong resided on Warren Street with her husband until about 1901. Miss Brown herself was an avid Keyport historian and kept much of the data that is contained in this book.

Keyport Steamboat Co.

ON AND AFTER MAY 3, 1897,

THE STEAMER MAGENTA

Will leave Keyport at 7 o'clock A. M., and returning leave New York, from pier 57, (old number), North River, foot of Hewitt avenue, West Washington Market, two blocks below West 14th street, at 4 P. M. Daily, except Saturdays and Sundays; Saturdays, at 3 P. M.

Single fare, 30c.; Excursion, 50c.

Also connecting at Keyport with street cars for Matawan. Single fare, 35c.; Excursion, 60c. Tickets for sale on boat and street cars.

A. F. WALLING, Agent.